Big Brother, Little Brother

Thank you to my friend, Charles Levi, who had a positive outlook on everything and loved his family and friends like nobody I'd ever seen before. The world needs more people like you. You will be greatly missed.

Thank you to my boys, who inspired the book. No one else will ever know the strength of my love for you. After all, you are the only ones who know what my heart sounds like from the inside. I promise to always love you unconditionally.

CRW Creations
Author: Dana Wilson
Illustrator: QBN Studios
Editor: Lianne March
Book Designer, Editor, and Rhyme and Meter Expert: Andrea Ketchelmeier
Photo credit: Caitlin Mares - Caitlin Rose Photography
Text Copyright © 2023 CRW Creations. First Edition. All rights reserved.
No part of this publication may be reproduced or distributed in any form or by any means without written consent from the publisher.
Library of Congress Control Number: 2023915385
ISBN 979-8-9869171-0-8 (Hardback)
ISBN 979-8-9869171-1-5 (Paperback)
ISBN 979-8-9869171-2-2 (eBook)
Send any inquiries to: siblingconnectionbooks@gmail.com

This book belongs to

_____

No matter what we choose to do,
It's ALWAYS fun when I'm with you!

I like it when we run and play.
We make up new games every day.

Our walkie-talkies are great fun.
We talk for hours in the sun...

Then grab our bikes and ride and ride.
I LOVE the days we spend outside!

We **work together** on the chores—
To wash the dishes and the floors.

It's easy when we both help out,
'Cause that's what **teamwork's** all about!

I like it when we cook and bake—
Especially when it's chocolate cake!

But I'd make ANYTHING with you.
Mom and Dad can help us too!

We love to SPLASH and play pretend.
I wish our baths would never end.

We laugh together as we scrub,
While popping bubbles in the tub.

I promise that you're safe and sound,
And nothing scary will be found.

Remember that I'm ALWAYS near,
And if you need me, I'll be here.

Those times when we get mad and fight,
We'll ask how we can make it right.

When one of us does something wrong,
Forgiving doesn't take too long.

Whenever I forget to share,
Remember that I always care.

Even if we disagree,
I'm here for you; you're here for me.

About the Author: Dana Wilson

Dana Wilson is a mommy to three wonderful boys: 9, 7, and 4. Her household practices respectful parenting, which prioritizes the parent-child relationship above all else. During a season when her boys were struggling to connect, she sought out resources to help them. When she couldn't find many books on sibling relationships, she was inspired to write one. She also intends to publish additional books that target a variety of family dynamics.

Dana started the Sibling Connection Books series because she believes that it is essential for every child to feel connected. Her hope is to empower all children with valuable skills and life lessons, and also teach them love, empathy, compassion, and how to connect with others. Parents can use this book to lead into meaningful discussions about connection, and siblings can read it to each other to strengthen their bond. The goal is for our kids to build long lasting relationships with each other.

Another one of Dana's passions is supporting other mothers and encouraging them to bring their desires and dreams to life. When she was looking for places to promote her book, she could not find many resources, so she decided to start her own Facebook group where moms can support other moms' businesses (their dreams). If you have your own passion you'd like to promote or if you just love supporting small businesses as a buyer, please join:

@MomsSupportingMomBusiness

Dana also invites you to join her Facebook support group to discuss ways to improve the parent-child relationship, and gain tips and advice to help strengthen your children's sibling relationships:

@RelationshipFocusedParenting

To follow Dana on social media, search Sibling Connection Books on Facebook, Instagram, Pinterest, and Youtube. You can find her website at www.siblingconnectionbooks.com and can email her at siblingconnectionbooks@gmail.com.

About the Illustrator: QBN Studios

QBN Studios is a small illustration studio located in Vernon, Connecticut. Owners Quynh Nguyen and Christopher MacCoy are passionate about helping authors fulfill their dreams and bring their words to life.

QBN Studios' goal is to create an immersive experience for their audiences to tumble headfirst into imaginary worlds.

Follow them on Instagram for the latest updates on illustrations, books, and other projects:

📷 @qbnstudios

Learn More About Consciously Parenting Through Connection

Parenting with connection prioritizes the parent-child relationship, utilizing tools derived from a variety of positive parenting resources. All behavior a child exhibits is communication, and connection is a child's greatest need. When children don't feel connected, they tend to show their emotions through their behavior. Increased connection is helpful in nearly every situation, and the parent-child relationship is the backbone for our children's healthy growth and development. Pam Leo and Rebecca Thompson Hitt are two amazing resources on the subject.

Pam Leo

Pam Leo is the author of Connection Parenting. After her first child was born in 1972, it became her passion to understand human behavior. Pam began to study child development, psychology, sociology, and anthropology. She wanted to learn why we are each born as a tiny innocent being, and some of us grow up to be a Mahatma Gandhi while others become an Adolf Hitler. What determines the difference? She was determined to find out.

Her journey has been and continues to be a wondrous one. While raising her two daughters, she supported them by being a family child care provider for children ages two to ten, fifty hours a week, fifty weeks a year, for twenty-two years. During that time she homeschooled her daughters and continued her own independent study of human development. In 1989 she developed the seven-session parenting series, "Meeting the Needs of Children," which she taught publicly and in the prison system with inmate parents.

The feedback she most often gets from parents is, "I wish I'd had this information from the beginning." In response to this feedback, she created a prenatal parenting class. She became certified as a childbirth educator and as a doula as preparation to teach her new class. The "Bonding with Your Baby" class draws from the works of Joseph Chilton Pearce, Jean Liedloff, Ashley Montagu, and James Prescott. The class focuses on supporting expectant parents in creating the best possible foundation for a strong parent-child bond.

If she had to put into one sentence all that she has learned about optimal human development and parenting, it would be this: our effectiveness as parents is in direct proportion to the strength of the bond we have with our child. Securing and maintaining that bond is our primary work as parents and is the key to optimal human development.

Her passion to learn how to support optimal human development grew into a mission to share all she had learned. In addition to teaching her classes, she has been sharing this information through her "Empowered Parents" column in the Parent & Family paper in Maine since 1994. When one of her articles was reprinted in the Empathic Parenting Journal, she was invited to work with the group of people who have now become the Alliance for Transforming the Lives of Children.

It's been a dream come true for her to have the opportunity to work in person with many of the people who have unknowingly been her mentors. Their common bond is their passion for and dedication to working together to make this information available to all people who either raise children or impact the lives of children. She can think of no work more worthy of her time, energy, resources, and love.

 You can find more information on Pam's website: connectionparenting.com

Rebecca Thompson Hitt

Rebecca Thompson Hitt, MS, MFT, is the founder of Consciously Parenting. She has been working with children and families for over 30 years. She's written 3 parenting books and will soon publish her 4th book called "It's Never Too Late to Heal". She is the founder and executive director of The Consciously Parenting Project, LLC, which she founded in 2007. She supports families with children of all ages around the world with educational resources, community groups, workshops, and retreats. She also has a two-year training program for parents and professionals to support a deepening understanding of relationship-focused parenting. She's the mother of two young adult sons and lives together with her sons and husband in Oaxaca, Mexico, where they love eating tacos and are trying to learn Spanish.

Consciously Parenting started as an idea when Rebecca's first son was born. There were so many parenting decisions that needed to be made and she wanted to make the best decisions she could for him, but parenting information was confusing and overwhelming even in 1998. With a deep interest in the attachment research, she set out to understand what the ingredients are for healthy relationships and how to change dysfunctional family patterns so that everyone in the family can heal together. She found that the key is focusing on the relationship, rather than the behaviors, and paying attention to the communication behind the behaviors. She went on to study prenatal and perinatal somatic psychology, which only deepened her understanding of how the body shows the story of what's happened to us beginning even before conception, and to our ancestors and how our behaviors communicate so much more than we understand on the surface. Consciously Parenting has an international following and Rebecca has trained people from over 15 countries around the world. This growing movement is about creating connection one family at a time.

You can learn more about The Consciously Parenting Project and offerings by visiting her website: consciouslyparenting.com

If you enjoyed this book, will you please take a moment to leave a review on Amazon, Goodreads, and/or my website: siblingconnectionbooks.com? Reviews are so very appreciated and can help your favorite stories succeed.

Please feel free to message me if you have any questions or want to share your own sibling connection story. I would love to hear about it.

Do you want this story to be read at your school? Ask your teacher or principal to email me to schedule a reading: siblingconnectionbooks@gmail.com

Thank you for your support!
-Dana Wilson

Made in the USA
Monee, IL
10 November 2023